BODY OF EVIDENCE
DVD STUDY
QUESTIONS

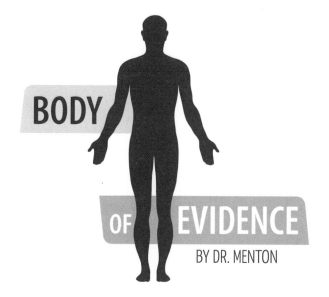

BODY

OF EVIDENCE

BY DR. MENTON

1:1
answersingenesis
Petersburg, Kentucky, USA

ISBN: 1-60092-427-1

Second Edition: November 2011
Second printing: April 2012

Printed in China

www.answersingenesis.org

CONTENTS

INTRODUCTION

About Dr. Menton

Your teacher, David Menton, PhD, brings thirty-four years of experience teaching both gross anatomy and microscopic anatomy to medical and graduate students at one of America's premier medical schools. Over the years, Dr. Menton has won numerous awards from his students for his teaching ability. This, together with his research on various organs of the body including skin, bone, kidney, and the placenta, makes him well-suited to share not just facts, but real insight into the marvels of the human body. However, the beginning student of human biology should not be intimated by Dr. Menton's postgraduate level teaching experience. Dr. Menton has a gift for explaining things in an understandable way as well as having a well-developed sense of humor.

Dr. Menton Describes His Approach to Learning Human Biology

Our body is truly a "body of evidence" for an all-knowing and all-powerful Creator. In this course of study we give credit to our Creator and Savior and recognize our accountability to Him.

> Know that the Lord, He is God; it is He who has made us, and not we ourselves; we are His people and the sheep of His pasture (Psalm 100:3).

Biology is the one science course that every high school graduate is expected to have studied. About one-third of a typical biology textbook is devoted to human biology. *Body of Evidence* seeks to give the home-educated (or Christian school) student personal instruction in this important field of science. I see the role of the teacher as not simply to give a list of facts for the student to memorize, but rather to share real insights based on experience, and to motivate the student to pursue a lifetime of learning.

For the beginning student, human biology is best understood with a combined structural (anatomical) and functional (physiological) approach. It has been said that structure and function are "two sides of the same coin," but I believe they are the very substance of the same coin. They simply cannot be totally separated since either by itself is meaningless.

Attempting to understand even the basic structure and function of the human body is a daunting task. I have found that this task is made easier if we begin with an understanding of the four primary tissues that make up all the organs of our body: epithelium, connective tissue, muscle, and nerve. *Body of Evidence* begins with a survey of these primary tissues, and then builds on this understanding as each of several organ systems of the body is described in terms of its primary tissues.

While there is much that can be learned from gross anatomy (what can be seen with the unaided eye), experience has taught me that structure and function come together best at the microscopic level of observation. For example, relatively little can be learned about the structure and function of the kidney at the gross anatomical level, but at the microscopic level it begins to reveal its secrets. Throughout *Body of Evidence* we turn again and again to the light and electron microscopes to understand something of the structure and function of some of the marvelous organs of our body.

Only so much can be learned from watching videos and reading books about the human body—the most exciting learning happens when the student looks for himself or herself at real organs and tissues. While it is unlikely that the beginning student will have an opportunity to study a real human body at the gross anatomical level, it is quite possible to study human organs and tissues (as well as those from various mammals) at the microscopic level. Suitable microscopes can be purchased for about $200 and prepared microscope slides can be purchased for a nominal price from various sources. A microscope and about ten carefully chosen slides could greatly enhance the learning experience of a student studying *Body of Evidence*.

Study Tips

It is typical for a video instruction course of this type to include a detailed outline of the course. But outlines are something that interested students can easily generate on their own. For this course I have chosen to provide instead a series of questions that direct the student's interest to find answers. These questions follow the order in which topics are presented so that in their own way they serve as an outline. More importantly, the questions direct the student to look for the unfolding answers as they watch the video.

I suggest that the student read over the entire question/outline for each part before watching the DVD. This will serve as a "pretest" that will give students a sense of what they already know as well as a sense of what they are about to learn. You may want to watch an entire part without consulting the question/outline so as not to disrupt the flow of the lecture, but it is strongly recommended that you also go through each part by first reading each question then watching the video for the answer. Be aware that a complete answer to a question may unfold later than when the topic is first introduced. It will be of considerable help if you are able to conveniently start and stop the DVD so you can read each question just before it is covered. Space is provided in this Study Questions guide for you to write your answers.

After completing each part, the student should read through the questions again and attempt to answer them without the video. The parent or teacher may wish to select questions for use as an exam. You will find an answer key to each of the lessons at www. bodyofevidence.org.

Students are encouraged to supplement the information they learn from the videos with other sources such as biology textbooks and on websites such as http://en.wikipedia.org and http://health.howstuff works.com/human-body/systems. I urge the student to visit the *Body of Evidence* website at www. bodyofevidence.org for additional information tailored especially for the needs of those studying *Body of Evidence*. This website will also be used to correct the occasional misspeaks and errors that crept into *Body of Evidence*.

Acknowledgments

I wish to acknowledge and thank Dan Zordel and Dale Mason of Answers in Genesis in Petersburg, KY, and the video production team at American Family Association in Tupelo, MS, for all their assistance in making *Body of Evidence* possible. Finally, I want to thank my "favorite students" Anna Beth and Matthew who sat through four long days of videotaping with unflagging attention.

CELLS & TISSUES

Part One

1. What does the word anatomy mean?

2. What is gross anatomy, and how does regional gross anatomy differ from systemic gross anatomy?

3. What is histology and where does the word come from?

4. How does a compound microscope differ from a stereo microscope?

5. What is ultrastructural anatomy?

6. Who named the biological cell and why did he give it this name?

7. How do plant cells differ from animal cells?

8. About how many cells are in the human body?

9. How many primary tissues make up the body?

10. A dime is approximately how thick in the metric system?

11. What is the unit of measurement we typically use when studying something under the microscope? How big is this unit compared to the thickness of a dime?

12. What unit of measurement is useful when studying specimens under the electron microscope?

13. What is meant by the term optical resolution?

14. What is the resolution of the unaided human eye?

11:06 15. What is the best resolution of the compound light microscope and how does this compare to that of the electron microscope?

16. What is the approximate diameter of a red blood cell?

17. What is the approximate size of the banding period of skeletal muscle fibers?

18. How thick are most sections of tissues we study under the light microscope?

19. What is fixation and why is this important?

20. What is imbedding and why is this important?

21. What kind of instrument is used to cut sections for microscopic study?

22. Why do we stain sections for study under the microscope?

23. Briefly describe the structure and function of the nucleus and nucleolus.

24. What is the function of ribosomes?

25. What does the presence of a large amount of rough endoplasmic reticulum tell us about a cell? How does this differ from a cell that has mostly free ribosomes?

26. What are some of the functions of the Golgi apparatus of the cell?

27. What are mitochondria and what is their function?

28. What are lysosomes and what is their function?

29. What do centrioles do?

30. What are HeLa cells and why are they unusual?

31. What is the difference between a transmission electron microscope and a scanning electron microscope?

32. What is the benefit of using a scanning electron microscope over a light microscope besides greater magnifying power?

33. What are the four primary tissues that make up our body?

34. What are the distinctive characteristics of epithelial tissue?

35. What is the difference between a simple squamous epithelium and a stratified squamous epithelium?

36. List six functions of epithelium and describe an example of each.

37. What kind of epithelium lines the lumen of all blood vessels and why does this make sense?

38. What shape are cells in a simple epithelium when viewed from their surface rather than their edge?

39. What are the three basic ways you can arrange epithelial layers? Give an example of each.

40. What are goblet cells and where would we find them?

41. What is the difference between microvilli and cilia, where might we find each, and what is their function?

42. How do cilia beat and why is this important?

43. How may epithelia be arranged in glands?

Part Two

1. How does connective tissue differ from epithelia?

2. What is the main protein of connective tissue?

3. List four primary functions of connective tissue.

4. What are the two types of connective tissue proper?

5. What is the difference between regular and irregular dense connective tissue? Where would we find regular dense connective tissue?

6. Why is blood classified as a connective tissue?

7. What is the function of elastic connective tissue?

8. What are the supporting connective tissues?

9. What are the cells that make connective tissue fibers?

10. What is the function of macrophages?

11. What is the function of plasma cells?

12. What occupies the space between the fibers in loose connective tissue?

13. What are mast cells, what is their function, and where might we be most likely to find them?

14. Why do you think fibroblasts contain so much rough surface endoplasmic reticulum (rough ER)?

15. What is tropocollagen?

16. How can a connective tissue be stretchy when the collagen fibers that make it up are inelastic?

17. What is distinctive about the appearance of plasma cells when viewed with a microscope?

18. Why do you think plasma cells have so much rough ER?

19. Give two locations where we would expect to find irregular dense connective tissue. What function would this tissue serve in these locations?

20. Give two locations where we would find regular dense connective tissue. What function would this tissue serve in these locations?

21. What is the difference between a collagen fiber and a collagen fibril?

22. Can we see a collagen fibril under the light microscope?

23. What is adipose tissue and why do sections of it studied under the light microscope look like hollow bubbles?

24. What is the role of elastin in irregular dense connective tissue?

25. What is the function of the elastic membrane in arteries and where is it located?

26. What are the three types of muscle we find in our body, and how do these muscle cells differ from one another?

27. Give an example of where we would expect to find each of the three types of muscle.

28. What are the main functional differences between smooth muscle and skeletal muscle?

29. Why do the nuclei often have a "corkscrew" or wrinkled shape in highly contracted smooth muscle cells?

30. How many nuclei might we expect to find in a skeletal muscle cell? How does this differ from a smooth muscle cell?

31. Why do we call skeletal muscle cells/fibers a syncytium and how is this formed?

32. Where are the nuclei located in a skeletal muscle cell, and how does this differ from smooth and cardiac muscle cells?

33. What causes the banding in striated skeletal muscle?

34. What is a muscle fiber and how does it differ from a muscle fibril (myofibril)?

35. What is the function of the "T-tubule" system in skeletal muscle?

36. What is the function of the sarcoplasmic reticulum of skeletal muscle?

37. What is the sarcomere of a skeletal muscle fibril?

38. What is the function of the intercalated disks of cardiac muscle?

39. How do skeletal muscle cells attach to a tendon?

40. List some important differences between the central and peripheral nervous system?

41. What are the important differences between a nerve and a fiber tract and where would we find an example of each?

42. What are dermatomes?

43. What is the epineurium and what is it made of?

44. What is the endoneurium?

45. What is myelin and what is its function?

46. What is the Schwann cell and what is its function?

SKELETAL SYSTEM

Part One

1. What is a Warren truss?

2. Where do we find a biological example of a Warren truss?

3. What lesson do we learn from finding a "Warren truss" in nature?

4. How should we respond to skeptics who argue that the Bible is not a book of biology or geology and thus need not be taken seriously when it touches on these matters?

5. Where does the Bible say God made bones, ligaments, muscle, and skin?

6. What type of primary tissue is cartilage and bone?

7. Why is cartilage important to our understanding of bone?

8. Give five examples of cartilage in the adult human body.

9. Why is cartilage important in joints?

10. Give examples of bones that do not begin as cartilage in the embryo and fetus.

11. List the three distinctive cell types found in cartilage and describe their functions.

12. What is the difference between hypertrophic and hyperplastic?

13. What is the fate of most cartilage that forms in the embryo and fetus?

14. What are the constituents of cartilage matrix and what purpose to they serve?

15. What is the difference between calcified cartilage and bone?

16. What is the function of calcified cartilage?

17. What is the most unusual characteristic of cartilage and why is this important for the articular cartilage of joints?

18. What are the two ways that cartilage can grow and how does this differ from bone?

19. What is hyaline cartilage? Give an example in the body.

20. What is an isogenous nest in cartilage and what is its significance?

21. Where is articular cartilage found?

22. Where is elastic cartilage found and how does it differ from hyaline cartilage?

23. Give two locations where fibrocartilage is found and how does this cartilage differ from hyaline cartilage?

24. What are Sharpey's fibers?

25. Why do people often get a little shorter in stature as they reach old age?

26. How many bones are in the adult human body?

27. What is the largest bone in the body?

28. What are the three smallest bones in the body?

29. Give two other distinctive characteristics of the three smallest bones in the body.

30. What is the difference between red marrow and yellow marrow (other than color)?

31. Where do we find truly hollow (air-filled) bones in our body?

32. List five important functions of bones and give examples of each.

33. What organs are protected by our rib cage?

34. For muscles to move our body or its members they must cross at least one what?

35. What is the difference between the so-called "origin" and "insertion" of muscles on our bones?

36. Give three important functions for calcium outside of bone in our body.

37. How may calcium be released from bone?

Part Two

1. What is the difference between the blood supply of cartilage and bone?

2. What is the main difference in the metabolism of cartilage and bone?

3. What is the difference in the growth mechanism of cartilage and bone?

4. What is the difference in the mineral composition of cartilage and bone?

5. What is the difference in water content between cartilage and bone?

6. What chemical binds the water in cartilage?

7. What are the three main cell types in bone?

8. What is osteoid, what cell makes it, and why is it important?

9. Why can't osteocytes divide to produce more cells?

10. What is the function of the osteoclast?

11. What is osteopetrosis and why does it result in anemia?

12. How might osteopetrosis be cured?

13. What is the difference between the periosteum and the endosteum?

14. In what sense can it be said that we never get over 15 years old?

15. How long do red blood cells last before they are replaced in our body?

16. What purpose is served by the repeated removal of adult bone by osteoclasts and replacement of bone by osteoblasts?

17. What is the difference between osteoporosis and osteopetrosis?

18. What is the function of calcified cartilage in the development and growth of bone?

19. How do osteoclasts manage to become so large compared to osteoblasts?

20. How does the osteoclast dissolve the mineral of bone?

21. How does the osteoclast dissolve the collagen of bone?

22. What is a Howship's lacuna?

23. What is an osteon and how is it formed?

24. What is a Haversian canal?

25. What are the two basic components of bone?

26. In what form is the calcium of bone?

27. What is a composite material and how is bone an example of a composite?

28. What is endochondral ossification?

29. What is the growth plate of bone, where is it located, and how is it formed?

30. Why is a cartilage growth plate essential for the growth in length (but not width) of long bones?

31. What stimulates the growth of cartilage in the growth plate?

32. What is the eventual fate of the growth plate as we reach our adult height?

33. What causes the disease acromegaly and what are its symptoms?

34. How does gigantism differ from acromegaly in cause and symptoms?

35. What is the difference in location, structure, and function between compact bone and spongy bone?

36. The designer of the Eiffel Tower based its design on what part of what bone of the body?

37. What is the effect of bone modeling or remodeling on trabecular (spongy) bone?

38. What are the Volkmann's canals and how do they differ from Haversian canals?

39. Do osteons grow from the inside out or the outside in?

40. How does a new osteon form within existing compact bone?

41. How do the osteocytes in an osteon get their oxygen and nutrition?

42. Living bone can change its shape and size in response to loads (or lack of load) placed upon it. One theory for how this is accomplished is the piezoelectric theory. What components of bone are involved in this and how might this work?

43. Why do astronauts often lose bone mass when they spend a long time in space?

44. Describe the mechanism by which bone fractures are healed.

45. Why is it important to put a healing bone fracture in a cast?

INTEGUMENTARY SYSTEM

Part One

1. What is the largest organ in the body and about how much would it weigh in an adult?

2. How long would we be likely to live if we suddenly lost the thin dead layer on the surface of our skin?

3. List eight functions of skin and briefly describe each function and the parts of the skin involved.

4. What are the three basic layers of the skin?

5. What is the main component of the dermis?

6. What is the main component of the hypodermis?

7. What skin structures extend down into the hypodermis?

8. What is the name of the important dead layer on the surface of our epidermis?

9. What is the function of the retinaculum cutis?

10. What is the difference between tight skin and loose skin? Give examples of each.

11. What are the two basic types of skin in our body? Give examples of each.

12. In what sense is our dermis a "fabric"?

13. What are Langer's lines and how were they demonstrated?

14. What is the function of the weave and elastic fibers of the skin?

15. What happens to the elasticity of skin as we get older?

16. How is it possible that many brilliant scientists seem to fail to see the design in our body?

17. What are the main structural and functional differences between thin skin and thick skin?

18. List the three main layers of the living epidermis and describe the distinctive structure and function of each.

19. What makes keratin in our epidermis, hair, and fingernails so strong?

20. What is melanin and where is it produced?

21. What are the two layers of the dermis and what are the distinctive functions of each?

22. How does the papillary dermis function in controlling blood pressure and body temperature?

23. What is the function of Meissner's corpuscles and where do we find them?

24. What route do sweat gland ducts take through the epidermis and where do they emerge on thick skin?

25. What are the two most important functions of sweat?

26. What is the location and function of programmed cell death (apoptosis) in the skin?

27. What are corneocytes?

28. How do the corneocytes of thick skin and thin skin differ?

29. Normally, where does all the cell division occur in the epidermis?

30. Why must the rate of cell division in the living epidermis precisely match the rate of the loss of dead cells from the stratum corneum?

31. Approximately how much dead skin (corneocytes) does an adult shed every year?

32. How are corneocytes arranged in the stratum corneum of thin skin?

33. What holds the corneocytes together in the stratum corneum?

34. How are the keratin filaments arranged in the corneocyte?

35. What is the apparent mechanism for producing the precisely stacked columns of corneocytes in thin skin?

Part Two

1. What gives the color (shade) to our skin?

2. Where do pigment cells (melanocytes) come from and when do they enter the skin?

3. Where do melanocytes reside in the skin?

4. What do melanocytes produce?

5. What are the relative numbers of melanocytes in black and white skin?

6. Melanocytes make melanin granules, but where do they go from there?

7. What kind of cancer can the sun cause in our skin?

8. What cells in the skin are susceptible to actinic radiation (sun)?

9. How are the cells that are susceptible to ultraviolet rays from the sun protected?

10. What accounts for the difference in pigmentation of darker and lighter skin?

11. Why are the pigment-producing cells lighter than the stem cells of the epidermis?

12. What cells get the pigment from the melanocytes?

13. Epidermal cells that do not get the pigment from the melanocytes are engaged in what important function?

14. Why is the pigment in the basal cells of the epidermis likened to an umbrella?

15. What shape are melanocytes?

16. What are the steps in getting pigment from the melanocytes to a supranuclear cap in the epidermal stem cell?

17. How do we get all the different shades in the skin of humans given that we all come from Adam and Eve?

18. How many sweat glands do we have in the skin?

19. How much sweat can our sweat glands produce?

20. What are the functions of sweat?

21. How does a dog adjust body temperature?

22. What other creatures besides humans sweat enough to regulate their body temperature?

23. Where do we find sweat glands in all mammals?

24. How do apocrine sweat glands differ from eccrine sweat glands? Where do we find them in humans?

25. Why does apocrine sweat often have a strong odor?

26. What is in eccrine sweat besides water?

27. The secretory part of sweat glands, like all glands, is located in what specific type of primary tissue? Why?

28. Compare the microscopic anatomy of eccrine and apocrine sweat glands.

29. Where are the sebaceous (oil) glands of the skin located and where do they secrete their product?

30. Why is oil on the hair important for many mammals?

31. What is holocrine secretion?

32. What are the three basic types of hairs and how do they differ?

33. What type of hairs do we have on our nose and forehead, and why do we not generally notice them?

34. What are the first hair follicles to be formed on our body and when are these hairs normally shed?

35. How is it possible that we can become "bald" without losing a hair?

36. What type of tissue occupies the dermal papillae of the hair?

37. Where does the actual growth of the hair occur in the hair follicle?

38. What are the small muscles that attach to each hair follicle?

39. What is the difference between the cuticle cells and cortical cells of the hair shaft?

40. Why is the cuticle important for hair grooming?

41. About how much do our terminal hairs grow each day?

42. What is the hair growth cycle?

43. Why is it that most mammals do not need to get haircuts?

44. Why is it that some people are able to grow longer scalp hair than others?

45. Why do some dogs (like poodles) require haircuts while most dogs do not?

46. Why is it that the dogs that require haircuts are the dogs that don't shed hair?

47. What is the function of the cuticle that lines the hair follicle?

48. Why is the "hair lock" important?

49. When you pull a hair out of your scalp, what is the little bulge on the end of the hair?

50. How is the hair able to grow in length if it's locked in the follicle?

51. What is a blister?

52. What causes "goose bumps"?

53. What might be a function of the erector muscles of hair in humans?

54. What is the function of the facial skin muscles?

55. What two facial muscles are the most important and why?

CARDIOVASCULAR SYSTEM

Part One

1. How large should a normal heart be?

2. How much blood is in the adult body?

3. How many times does the heart beat per minute?

4. How much blood will the heart pump in an average lifetime?

5. What is the problem with the death of heart muscle cells (heart attack)?

6. Why must the heart be a dual pump and what are these two pumps?

7. Why does the blood "crisscross" between the two pumps?

8. Blood from where is returned through the superior vena cava?

9. Blood from where is returned through the inferior vena cava?

10. Where does blood returning from the lungs enter the heart?

11. Where does blood returning from the rest of the body enter the heart?

12. What is the basic difference in blood flow and the oxygen content of blood in most of the arteries and veins of the body, and how is this different in the case of the lungs?

13. How many veins (pulmonary veins) return blood to the heart from each lung?

14. Do the atria beat at the same time or at different times? Is this the same for the ventricles?

15. What is the name of the valve between the right atrium and right ventricle?

16. What prevents the valves of the ventricles from allowing blood to flow back into the atria (reflux) when the ventricle contracts?

17. What is the function of the papillary muscles of the ventricles?

18. Where does the blood go from the right ventricle? What is the name of this special vessel going to the lung?

19. Which has the thickest muscular wall, the ventricles or atria, and why does this make sense?

20. What is the name of the valve between the left atrium and left ventricle and why is it given this name?

21. Why is the muscular wall of the left ventricle so much thicker than that of the right ventricle?

22. What causes the "lub-dub" sound you hear when you listen to the heart with a stethoscope?

23. What is the ligamentum arteriosum and what does it develop from?

24. Evolutionists believe in "vestigial structures" (such as the "tailbone") as proof of evolution. Why is the ligamentum arteriosum a true vestigial structure, but the "tailbone" is not at all a vestige of evolution?

25. Why is it important that the heart be inside a lubricated pericardial sac?

26. What is the difference between a visceral layer and a parietal layer?

27. Which is the most ventral (toward the front of the body), the right atrium or the left atrium?

28. What is the difference between the auricles and the atria?

29. What causes a heart attack?

30. Why do we call the arteries that supply the muscle of the heart "coronary" arteries?

31. What happens to heart muscle when it dies?

32. What happens to veins that are used to replace coronary arteries?

33. Why is it possible to transplant a heart but not an eye?

34. What is the effect of the sympathetic and the parasympathetic nervous system on the heart?

35. What happens to the heartbeat when a heart is transplanted and why?

36. What is the pacemaker of the heart?

37. Why must the heart contract from the bottom up?

Part Two

1. Why do some cardiologists deny that the heart shows any evidence of intelligent design? (Hint: it's not stupidity.)

2. How does striated cardiac muscle differ from striated skeletal muscle?

3. What are the Purkinje fibers of the heart?

4. What is a neurovascular bundle?

5. What type of artery is found close to the heart and why is this so?

6. What is systole and diastole?

7. What is the function of the muscular arteries, and what is the function of the muscle?

8. What is an arteriole?

9. What is a blood capillary and what is its function?

10. Approximately how long are all the capillaries of the body?

11. What is a postcapillary venule and what is its function?

12. What is the difference in structure and function of arteries and veins?

13. How does the blood get back to the heart within the veins?

14. What is unusual about the large arteries in the neck of the giraffe?

15. What is osmotic pressure?

16. What is the difference between blood plasma and tissue fluid?

17. What is unique about lymphatic vessels compared to blood vessels? What is their function?

18. How does lymph get into lymphatics?

19. What is meant by hypertonic, isotonic, and hypotonic solutions, and what effect does this have on red blood cells?

20. Describe the layers of the wall of a blood vessel.

21. What is special about the endothelium compared to almost all other epithelia?

22. What are the microscopic differences between an elastic artery, a muscular artery, and a vein?

23. What is distinctive about the structure of the arteriole compared to other arteries?

24. What is a mesentery?

25. Does the blood move faster in the vein or the artery?

26. Which typically has the largest lumen, an artery or vein?

27. How can you tell a large lymphatic from a vein in a neurovascular bundle?

28. How can you tell an artery from a vein in a neurovascular bundle?

29. In what way are lymphatics similar to veins in the lower part of the body?

30. What holds a lymphatic capillary open?

31. What causes a heart to become abnormally enlarged in some people?

32. When we exercise what makes our muscles get larger, more muscle cells or larger cells?

33. What effect does CPR have on the heart?

RESPIRATORY SYSTEM

Part One

1. What are the turbinates (or conchae) and what functions do they serve?

2. What is the function of the cartilage rings in the trachea?

3. Why are the tracheal "rings" actually horseshoe shaped?

4. What are the muscles between the ribs and what is their function?

5. What is the function of the ribs sloping down at an angle?

6. How many lobes does the left lung have and how many lobes does the right lung have?

7. What important organ resides in the mediastinum between the lungs?

8. Why is it important that the lungs reside in a double wall pleural sac?

9. What holds the lung open in its pleural space?

10. What is the most important muscle for breathing and where is it located?

11. What structures pass through the diaphragm?

12. What structures allow the ribs to move up and down?

13. What is involved in expelling air from the lung?

14. The muscles of breathing are voluntary muscles. Why might that surprise us?

15. When the diaphragm flattens out in breathing, what organs in the abdomen need to move out of the way?

16. The movement of the organs when the diaphragm flattens would produce heat of friction. How is this minimized?

17. What are the structures that branch off the trachea to supply air to each lung?

18. Why is it that if a child inhales (aspirates) a small structure like a bean, it is more likely to go into the right lung than the left lung?

19. All bronchi are kept open by what structures?

20. How do bronchioles differ from bronchi?

21. What structures are included in the respiratory system?

22. Where is the olfactory mucosa located and what does it do?

23. How does the size of the olfactory mucosa of humans compare to that of dogs?

24. Where are the pharynx and larynx located?

25. How are the turbinates able to heat the air we breathe?

26. Where is the olfactory mucosa located in the nasal cavity?

27. What is the function of odorant-binding proteins?

28. What would normally keep food and water from going down the trachea instead of the esophagus?

29. What is the advantage of having the trachea and esophagus meet in the oropharynx?

30. What are the tracheal rings made of?

31. What is the function of mucus lining much of the respiratory tree, and what cells make the mucus?

32. How is the mucus able to be moved up the respiratory tree to the oropharynx?

33. What movement is necessary for cilia to move mucus?

34. Mucus is too viscous to allow ciliary movement. How is this problem solved?

35. Describe the structure of the axoneme.

36. What makes the cilium bend and move?

Part Two

1. All bronchi have what primary tissue which is lacking in bronchioles?

2. How does an alveolar duct differ from a bronchiole?

3. What structure is necessary for gas exchange in the lung?

4. What is an alveolar sac?

5. Why must the alveolar wall be very thin?

6. What are greater alveolar cells (type two pneumocytes), how do they differ from type one pneumocytes, and what do they produce?

7. Why do babies who are born a few months premature have trouble breathing?

8. Why is surfactant important for breathing?

9. Why does warm water taste "flat" compared to cold water?

10. How is warm blood able to carry oxygen?

11. What is the shape of a red blood cell and why is this shape important?

12. What is the problem with red blood cells in sickle cell anemia?

13. How does the red blood cell keep its shape?

14. Why is the spleen removed sometimes in patients who have sickle cell anemia?

15. About how many different ways could you put the amino acids of hemoglobin together? How many are known to work normally?

16. What is the function of neutrophils and what do they look like?

17. What is the function of eosinophils and what do they look like?

18. What is the function of basophils and what do they look like?

19. What type of cells do monocytes turn into?

20. What are the two basic types of lymphocytes found in blood and what are their functions?

21. What are blood platelets and what is their function?

22. Where is blood normally made?

23. What is a megakaryocyte and what does it produce?

24. What are the stages of development of a red blood cell in the marrow?

25. What is the difference between an erythroblast and erythrocyte?

26. If you see immature red blood cells in peripheral blood, what might be causing the problem?

27. What problems does smoking cause in the lungs?

28. What is a lung lobule?

DIGESTIVE SYSTEM

Part One

1. What is the alimentary canal and approximately how long is it in the adult?

2. About how long is the small and large intestine?

3. The esophagus runs just behind what structure?

4. What structure must the esophagus pass through to reach the stomach?

5. What are the gastric rugae?

6. Where is the duodenum located?

7. What important digestive gland secretes into the duodenum?

8. What is the cecum?

9. What is mastication and what important functions does it accomplish?

10. What two basic activities does digestion accomplish?

11. What are the five major processes of digestion?

12. What is the gut associated lymphoid tissue (GALT)? Give some examples and functions.

13. What are the filiform papillae of the tongue and what is their function?

14. What are circumvalate papillae and what is their function?

15. What are taste buds and where are they located?

16. How could you demonstrate that smell is an important part of taste?

17. What is the odontogenic organ?

18. Why can the enamel of our teeth not be repaired or changed after it is formed?

19. What are the ameloblasts, where are they located, and what is their function?

20. What are the three different mineralized materials in the tooth in order of their hardness?

21. Why is it important that there be a layering of progressive hardness in these tooth materials?

22. What cells produce dentin and where are they located?

23. Why do we produce secondary teeth and what do they develop from?

24. What makes up the pulp of the tooth and what is its function?

25. Why is dentin able to repair itself but not enamel?

26. What material of the tooth is most like bone and how is it similar?

27. What is the primary function of cementum?

28. What is the periodontal ligament, where is it located, and what are its functions?

29. What is one of the few areas of the body where we find a free edge on an epithelium?

30. Why is the periodontal ligament susceptible to contamination by bacteria and what normally prevents it?

31. Why is it we can't see the enamel in a typical section of the tooth and its gum?

32. How does the angle of the fibers in the periodontal ligament change as we go down into the tooth socket? Why is this important?

33. How is the periodontal ligament anchored to the tooth and its bony socket?

34. How is the growth of a tooth similar to the growth of bone?

35. How does tetracycline help us to understand how the tooth grows?

36. Which of the dental hard tissues contains the most organic material and which contains the most inorganic mineral?

Part Two

1. What are the three major salivary glands and where are they located?

2. How do the secretary products of the three salivary glands differ? Why is this useful?

3. What is a serous acinus and how does it differ from a mucous acinus?

4. Acinus means "grape-like." Why is this a good name for the glandular elements of the parotid gland?

5. Where are the minor salivary glands located and what are their functions?

6. What do the esophageal glands secrete and what is its function?

7. List the seven layers of the wall that are found throughout the tubes of the digestive system and briefly describe each.

8. What is peristalsis, what layers of the wall of the intestinal tract is responsible for this, and what is its function?

9. What is the nerve supply that controls peristalsis in the gut and why is this important?

10. What is the largest collection of ganglion cells outside the brain?

11. What kind of muscle do we find in the stomach and in the small and large intestine?

12. How is the muscle in the wall of the esophagus different from the intestines?

13. Describe the difference in the upper, middle, and lower third of the esophagus. Why is this useful?

14. What kind of epithelium lines the esophagus? Why is this useful?

15. What are the functions of the stomach?

16. What substances does the stomach secrete and what is the function of each?

17. What is pepsin?

18. What is chyme?

19. What is the function of the pyloric valve and where is it located?

20. What is the function of bile and where is it produced?

21. What are the major cell types in the stomach gastric glands and what is the function of each?

22. What is a stomach ulcer?

23. How are the parietal cells of the gastric glands able to produce hydrochloric acid without destroying the cells themselves?

24. What do the chief cells of the gastric glands produce?

25. What are the three major parts of the intestine?

26. What is the mesentery of the intestine and what is its function?

27. What is unique about the lining of the small intestine and what is its function?

28. When lipids are absorbed in the small intestine, what vessel do they enter?

29. What is the difference between villi and microvilli and what functions do they serve?

30. Where is bile produced and what is its function?

31. What is the main function of the large intestine?

32. What are the three chief parts of the large intestine?

33. What causes diarrhea?

34. What are the crypts of Lieberkuhn and what is their function?

35. Why is it important that the number of goblet cells increase as we progress through the large intestine?

36. What are the two major accessory glands of the digestive system and what are their functions?

37. Where does the pancreas release its enzymes?

38. What is the difference between an endocrine gland and an exocrine gland?

39. What is the endocrine gland of the pancreas and what does it secrete?

40. What do the exocrine cells of the pancreas secrete?

41. Blood leaving the intestine goes to what important organ?

42. What is a portal system?

43. What is the function of the gall bladder?

44. What are some of the functions of the liver?

45. What is the Kupffer cell and what are its functions?

46. Where is the appendix located?

47. Evolutionists insist that the appendix is a useless evolutionary vestige of the cecum. What is wrong with this argument?

48. Recent research suggests what important function for the appendix?

49. What is the problem with declaring any organ of the body to be without function?

50. What is the function of salivary amylase?

URINARY SYSTEM

Part One

1. Where are the kidneys located and why is this important?

2. Why are they referred to as being retroperitoneal?

3. Where are the kidneys located in the developing fetus?

4. Where do the testes begin in the developing fetus?

5. The mature kidney receives its blood and returns blood to what major vessels?

6. What organ sits on top of the kidney?

7. What is the function of the ureter?

8. What is the function of the urethra?

9. Why are there two ureters but only one urethra?

10. Where is the prostate gland located in males?

11. What is the normal osmotic concentration of blood and of urine (measured in milliosmoles)?

12. What is meant by hypertonic and hypotonic?

13. What are the three basic functions of the kidney?

14. What is urea?

15. List five things that the kidney does for us that are essential for life?

16. What hormone produced by the kidney is necessary for proper red blood cell concentration in our blood?

17. What is the hollow space in the kidney?

18. Approximately how much blood enters the kidney each day and how much is filtered as ultrafiltrate?

19. Approximately how much of the blood entering the kidney is reabsorbed?

20. What is the typical daily urine output for an adult?

21. The kidney not only filters on the basis of size, but what else?

22. What things are normally not permitted to pass through the urinary filter?

23. What would be the problem if the kidney did not engage in reabsorption?

24. Why does the kidney also need to engage in secretion?

25. What is a renal lobe?

26. Is the renal pyramid a part of the cortex or the medulla?

27. How many nephrons are in the adult human's kidneys?

28. Each lobe feeds its urine into what structure?

29. What is the renal pelvis?

30. Trace the path of urine starting with a renal pyramid all the way through to the bladder.

31. Trace the blood passing through a kidney lobe starting with the interlobar artery and ending with the interlobar vein.

Part Two

1. What is a nephron?

2. Describe the arterial portal system of the nephron. What is its function?

3. Where does the important process of filtration occur in the nephron?

4. If you were to clean your house the way the kidney (nephron) "cleans" the blood of unwanted things, how would you do it?

5. List the different parts of the nephron beginning with the renal corpuscle.

6. Where are all the renal corpuscles located?

7. Where are all the proximal and distal convoluted tubules of the kidney?

8. What structures are located in the renal pyramid?

9. What is the function of the loop of Henle?

10. How does the osmolality (osmotic concentration in osmoles) vary within the renal pyramid?

11. What is the function of the "salt sink" in the renal pyramid? How does this involve the collecting duct?

12. What hormone affects the permeability of the collecting duct?

13. Why are we unable to survive by drinking seawater?

14. How are Mallard ducks able to survive on seawater?

15. What is a renal lobule?

16. What are glomerular capillaries?

17. What do we call the cells that make up the visceral layer that closely invests the glomerular capillaries of Bowman's capsule? Why are they given this name?

18. What is the structure of the ultrafilter in the renal corpuscle?

19. Describe the three layers of the renal filter.

20. What is the estimated pore size of the slit diaphragm?

21. What goes on in the proximal convoluted tubule?

22. What goes on in the loop of Henle?

23. What goes on in the distal convoluted tubule?

24. What is the concentration of the urine (ultrafiltrate) entering the collecting duct?

25. How does the structure of the lumen of the proximal convoluted tubule differ from that of the distal convoluted tubule?

26. How is blood pressure controlled in the kidney?

27. Why do we see so many mitochondria in the proximal and distal convoluted tubules?

28. Why is it difficult to see the cell membranes ("walls") of the cells in the convoluted tubules?

29. What effect does antidiuretic hormone (ADH) have on the walls of the collecting ducts in the renal pyramid?

30. What challenges do the lining cells (transitional epithelium) face?

THE HEARING EAR & THE SEEING EYE

Part One (Ear)

1. Why is it that many intelligent scientists deny the intelligent design of the ear and eye?

2. How does sound travel through the air to get to our ears?

3. What are the three basic parts of the ear and how is sound conducted in each?

4. Why is a liquid (mainly water) necessary in the inner ear?

5. How are wax and dead skin cells removed from the outer ear canal?

6. What is the function of the auricle of the ear?

7. What are the three bones of the middle ear?

8. What is the function of the small bones in the middle ear?

9. Why is it we often don't recognize our own voice when we are recorded?

10. How much does the eardrum have to move for us to hear a quiet sound?

11. What is the vistibulocochlear system?

12. What is the function of the semicircular canals and how is it accomplished?

13. What is the function of the saccule of the inner ear and how does it work?

14. What does the word cochlea mean and why is it appropriate?

15. What is the organ of Corti and how is it arranged in the cochlea?

16. What are the functions of the oval window and the round window of the cochlea?

17. How does the organ of Corti function to produce electrical signals from sound?

18. What is the structure and function of the tectorial membrane?

19. How does loud sound damage our hearing?

20. How does wiggling the "hairs" of the hair cells produce electrical signals that our brain can interpret as sound?

21. How high pitched a sound can young people normally hear?

22. Why is it occasionally necessary to put tubes through the eardrum?

23. Why is it important that the air pressure be the same on both sides of the eardrum?

24. What structure of the ear serves to equalize the pressure on both sides of the eardrum?

25. How does yawning often clear the pressure in our ears?

Part Two (Eye)

1. How widespread in the animal kingdom are "camera" eyes similar to what we see in humans?

2. How does the cornea differ from the sclera (whites) of the eye?

3. The cornea and lens have the same embryonic origin as what other organ we have studied?

4. The eye and optic tract (excluding the lens and cornea) are actually part of what structure of the body?

5. What is the function of the iris diaphragm?

6. What did the children of Israel call the pupil of the eye?

7. The expression "you are the apple of my eye" comes from the Bible, but what is the original expression and what does it mean?

8. Why is our blink reflex so much faster than the knee-jerk reflex?

9. What is the function of the blink reflex and what causes it to occur?

10. What simple test can be done in an emergency to see if an accident victim might be dead?

11. What is the difference between the orbits of the human eye and the orbits of all apes and monkeys?

12. What are the four rectus muscles of the eye and what is their function?

13. What is the function of each of the two oblique muscles of the eye?

14. How does the superior oblique muscle of the eye differ in structure from the inferior oblique?

15. What are the two different axes of the eye and why are they different?

16. How is the control of our oblique muscles different from the control of our rectus muscles?

17. What purpose is served by the rotation of the eye with the oblique muscles?

18. What happens to our vision if all twelve muscles in our two eyes do not work in perfect coordination?

19. Why is the muscular action of looking up or down so much more complicated than looking left and right?

20. The embryonic development of the eye is another example of the "pushed in balloon" principle. What is formed from the inner layer, and what is formed from the outer layer?

21. How does the lens of the eye develop?

22. What are the two lenses of the eye and which of the two bends light the most?

23. How does the lens focus and how does this differ from the focusing mechanism of a camera?

24. What is the natural shape of the lens and would this be focused up close or at a distance?

25. How does the eye minimize spherical aberration when it is close-focused?

26. Why does reading or other close work often require more light than when our eyes are focused on a distant object?

27. How does the lens survive without blood vessels?

28. What is the function of the pigment in the iris?

29. What are lens fibers (prisms)?

30. Why does the human eye often fail to focus as we get older?

31. How does the anterior lens epithelium differ from the posterior lens epithelium?

32. What is the protein that fills the lens?

33. What keeps the lens prisms in a precise arrangement?

34. What is the difference between fiber tracks and nerves?

35. How are the muscles of the iris arranged?

36. Where is the iris diaphragm located in relationship to the cornea and lens?

37. What muscle focuses the eye and how is it attached to the lens?

38. What is the large gelatinous ball that fills the eyeball behind the lens and how was it formed?

39. What is the watery liquid in front of the lens, how is it produced, and what is its function?

40. Why must the interior of the eyeball be kept under constant pressure?

41. Why do evolutionists think the eye is poorly designed?

42. Give several reasons why the seemingly "upside down" nature of the retina is advantageous.

43. How does the Müller cell seem to solve the problem of the "upside down" retina?

44. We can only see things sharply with what small part of the retina, and why is this a good design for us?

45. About 5% of the blood vessels supplying the retina are on top of the retina and right in our path of vision. How are we able to avoid seeing these blood vessels in our vision?

46. What experiment can you do to actually see your own retinal vessels and why does this work?

47. Where are the tear glands (lachrymal glands) located?

48. How is the tear fluid removed from the surface of the eye?

49. Why must the tear fluid layer be maintained at a precise thickness?

50. What are the most important functions of tear fluid?

51. What keeps the tear fluid on the eye?

52. Why do we get bleary-eyed and the sniffles when we cry?

53. What makes people nearsighted or farsighted?

54. How does a detached retina relate to the embryological development of the eye?

Answers Education Online
(web-based courses)

Choose from six great online courses as low as $89

	APO 101 (instructor-based)	APO 111 (self-paced)
Completion Time	12 weeks in week-long segments	Up to 6 months at your own pace
Number of Lessons	14	14
Instructor Interaction	Discussion forums and via email	Via email as needed
"Office Hours" (Live Chats)	Yes	No
Forums	Required student interaction	No required student interaction
Online Quizzes	Yes	Yes
Written Assignments	Yes	Yes
Final Assignment	Student activity	Online test
Certificate of Completion	Yes	Yes
ACSI CEU Credits available	Yes	Yes
Course Cost	$159	$129

APO101 and APO111 present foundational creation apologetics. Each covers the following topics, plus important concepts in biology and geology.

- The relevance of creation to the gospel
- The incompatibility of evolution and the Bible
- Biblical and scientific support for a recent, six-day creation
- How to use logic to defend your faith
- The nature of Noah's Flood
- Compromise in Christian doctrine
- Implications of death before sin
- The relationship between Genesis and the rest of the Bible
- The Seven C's of biblical history
- Basic radiometric dating concepts
- Understanding mutations and evolution

Those who pass the course can receive 4 ACSI-accredited Continuing Education Units (CEUs): 2 in biblical studies and 2 in educational studies.

Other courses include: (6 weeks / $89 ea.)
- APO 201—Creation Apologetics and the **Bible**
- APO 202—Creation Apologetics and **Biology**
- APO 203—Creation Apologetics and **Geology**
- APO 204—Creation Apologetics and **Astronomy**

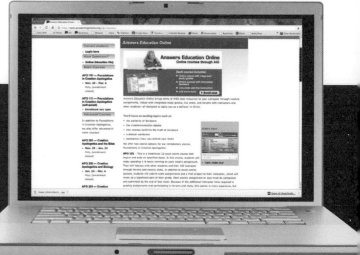

Excellent for anyone who wants to continue learning and to do so with built-in accountability. These courses bring some of AiG's best resources to your computer through web-based videos and reading assignments, integrated study guides, live chats, and forums with instructors and other students—all designed to equip you as a believer in Christ.

answerseducationonline.com